FUN and GAMES | DIVERSIÓN y JUEGOS

Everyday Play | ¡A diario!

WRITTEN BY • ESCRITO POR **Celeste Cortright**

ILLUSTRATED BY • ILUSTRADO POR **Sophie Fatus**

TRANSLATED BY • TRADUCIDO POR **María A. Pérez**

Barefoot Books
step inside a story

It's time to play! Let's laugh and learn.
Join in the fun and take a turn.

¡Es hora de jugar! Vamos a reír y aprender.
Únete a la diversión y espera tu turno.

In **hide-and-seek**, the counting down
Will send us running all around.
We find a clever hiding spot.
Here they come, ready or not!

En el juego del **escondite**, la cuenta atrás
nos pondrá a correr por todos lados.
Hallamos un buen escondite.
Aquí vienen, ¡listos o no!

Let's have some fun with **dominoes!**
We'll place them carefully in rows.
We try to find a matching tile,
Or else we draw one from the pile.

¡Vamos a divertirnos con el **dominó**!
Ponemos las fichas con cuidado en hileras.
Tratamos de encontrar una ficha igual.
Si no, tomamos una de la pila.

Hoop rolling is a timeless game.
To keep them upright is our aim!
We guide the rim with hooks or sticks,
And sometimes try out fancy tricks.

El **aro** es un juego que no pasa de moda.
¡Mantenerlo en pie es nuestro objetivo!
Guiamos el aro con ganchos o palillos,
y a veces hacemos elaborados trucos.

A **dollhouse** is a special toy
That everybody can enjoy.
We role-play while we all explore,
With action figures, dolls and more.

La **casa de muñecas** es un juguete especial
que todos pueden disfrutar.
Al explorar, hacemos representaciones
con figuras de acción, muñecas y más.

Let's take turns playing **spinning tops**.
We twirl the stem and then we watch!
The fast rotation helps them go
And keeps them balanced 'til they slow.

Vamos a turnarnos para jugar a los **trompos**.
¡Los hacemos girar y luego miramos!
La rotación rápida los hace seguir
y los balancea hasta que pierden velocidad.

With **tangrams**, we will try to make
An image out of seven shapes.
The puzzle's picture keeps evolving,
'Til we're finished problem-solving!

Con los **tangramas**, intentamos hacer
una imagen con siete figuras.
La imagen del rompecabezas va cambiando,
¡hasta que resolvemos el problema!

When we **jump rope** we skip our feet,
Then swing the rope and keep the beat.
We make small circles with our wrists,
And focus hard so no one trips!

Al **brincar la cuerda** alzamos los pies,
giramos la cuerda y mantenemos el ritmo.
Hacemos pequeños círculos con las muñecas,
¡y nos concentramos para que nadie tropiece!

Our **cuddly toys** are cherished friends
Who join us while we play pretend.
Throughout a day of highs and lows,
We have someone to snuggle close.

Nuestros **peluches** son amigos queridos
que se nos unen cuando jugamos a imaginar.
Durante todo un día de altibajos,
tenemos a alguien a quien abrazar.

We can be quiet or make noise
With lots of different games and toys.
We sometimes lose and sometimes win,
But most of all – we *all* join in!

Podemos estar callados o hacer ruido
con muchos juegos y juguetes diferentes.
A veces perdemos y a veces ganamos,
pero más que nada, ¡*todos* participamos!

Hide-and-Seek • Escondite

Hide-and-seek has been played
for as long as there have been
children. Igbo children in Nigeria
play a game called Oro, which
combines hide-and-seek
and the thrilling chase of
a game of tag!

El escondite se juega desde que
existen los niños. Los niños igbo
de Nigeria juegan algo llamado
Oro, que combina el escondite
con la divertida persecución de
un juego de . . . ¡el que la trae!

Dominoes • Dominó

The first form of dominoes came from China 1,000
years ago. There are many different games you can
play with these small tiles, by yourself or with friends.
Many games focus on matching up the numbers, but
you can also just line the tiles up and knock them over.

El primer tipo de dominó vino de China hace
1,000 años. Hay muchas formas de jugar
dominó, a solas o con amigos. Muchos juegos
se enfocan en formar parejas de números,
pero también puedes poner las piezas
paradas en hileras y tumbarlas.

Hoop Rolling • Aros

Hoops can be made of metal, vines, wood, bamboo and
many other materials. In ancient Egypt, hoops were
pushed around using plants called reeds.

Los aros se pueden hacer de metal, de tallos, de
madera, de bambú y de muchos otros materiales.
En el antiguo Egipto, los aros se
empujaban con cañas.

Dollhouses • Casa de muñecas

People have been creating dolls for thousands of
years, but the very first dollhouse (or doll's house) was
made over 600 years ago in Germany. Dollhouses were
originally created for adults to show off their collections
of miniatures.

Se hacen muñecas desde hace miles de
años, pero la primera casa de muñecas
(o casa para una muñeca) se
hizo hace 600 años en
Alemania. Al principio,
las casitas se creaban
para adultos que
exhibían sus
colecciones de
miniaturas.

Spinning Tops • Trompos

Some of the oldest spinning tops, possibly over 5,000 years old, were made of clay and found in Iraq. They can also be made from natural materials such as fruit, nuts and seeds.

Los trompos más antiguos, de hace unos 5,000 años, eran de arcilla y se hallaron en Iraq. También se hacen de materiales naturales como fruta, nueces y semillas.

Tangrams • Tangramas

Tangrams are seven flat shapes that, when put together, create a perfect square. Believed to have originally come from China, this puzzle game uses geometry, or the positioning of shapes, to solve problems.

Los tangramas son siete figuras planas que, cuando se juntan, forman un cuadrado perfecto. Se cree que vino de China. Este rompecabezas usa la geometría, o posicionamiento de las figuras, para resolver problemas.

Jump Ropes • Brincar la cuerda

The first jump ropes were made of vines and other natural materials. Also known as skipping ropes, they are popular all around the world both for fun and for exercise. A Japanese rope skipper once jumped over 150,000 times in 24 hours!

Las primeras cuerdas para brincar se hacían de tallos y otros materiales naturales. Al juego también se le dice "saltar la cuerda" o "la soga". La actividad es popular en todo el mundo como juego o ejercicio. ¡Una vez un japonés brincó más de 150,000 veces en 24 horas!

Cuddly Toys • Peluches

From our earliest days, cuddly toys give us comfort as we grow. The very first cuddly toys were made from bits of fabric then filled with straw. Known as rag dolls, they were created by the Romans thousands of years ago.

Desde que nacemos, algunos juguetes nos confortan a medida que crecemos. Los primeros peluches se hacían de trozos de tela rellenos de paja. Se llamaban muñecas de trapo, y los romanos las crearon hace miles de años.

To my cherished friends Eric and Iroh — C. C.

Para mis queridos amigos Eric e Iroh — C. C.

To Eden, my lovely niece, wishing her a life full of sweetness and fun — S. F.

Para Eden, mi bella sobrina, deseándole una vida llena de dulzura y diversión — S. F.

Barefoot Books
23 Bradford Street, 2nd Floor
Concord, MA 01742

Barefoot Books
29/30 Fitzroy Square
London, W1T 6LQ

First published in the United States of America by Barefoot Books,
Inc and in Great Britain by Barefoot Books, Ltd in 2020
This bilingual Spanish paperback edition first published in 2021

Graphic design by Sarah Soldano, Barefoot Books
Edited and art directed by Emma Parkin, Barefoot Books
Translated by María A. Pérez

Reproduction by Bright Arts, Hong Kong
Printed in China
This book was typeset in Barrio, Johann and Kidprint
The illustrations were prepared in mixed media
with acrylic paint, collage and digital paint

ISBN 978-1-64686-429-4

British Cataloguing-in-Publication Data:
a catalogue record for this book is available
from the British Library

Library of Congress Cataloging-in-Publication Data for the
English edition is available under LCCN 2020003028

3 5 7 9 8 6 4 2

The publisher would like to thank inclusivity specialist Anne Cohen for her expert review of this book.

La casa editorial le agradece a Anne Cohen, especialista en inclusividad, por su experto examen crítico de esta obra.